A BOOT UP

ISLE OF WIGHT PUBS

Phil Christian

First published in Great Britain in 2014

British Library Cataloguing-in-Publication Data
A CIP record for this title is available from the British Library

ISBN 978 0 85710 086 3

PiXZ Books
Halsgrove House, Ryelands Business Park,
Bagley Road, Wellington, Somerset TA21 9PZ
Tel: 01823 653777
Fax: 01823 216796
email: sales@halsgrove.com

An imprint of Halstar Ltd, part of the Halsgrove group of companies
Information on all Halsgrove titles is available at: www.halsgrove.com

Printed and bound in China by Toppan Leefung

Contents

	How to use this book	4
1	**Freshwater**	7
2	**Norton**	13
3	**Calbourne**	17
4	**Chale**	23
5	**Godshill**	29
6	**Arreton**	35
7	**Wootton**	41
8	**Newchurch**	47
9	**St Helen's**	53
10	**Bembridge**	59

How to use this book

The Island has around one pub for every square mile so satisfying your thirst is never going to be a major problem. The pubs can be found in all sorts of locations with many of them having lovely sea views or local historic landmarks. Many of them can be found in picturesque country villages and the vast majority of them serve excellent locally sourced, fresh food.

Add to this the fact that the Island has over 500 miles of footpaths and the only problem is knowing which paths take you to which pubs? This book has been carefully designed to help by describing in detail, 10 circular walks that combine a number of pubs in areas with local interest. This will hopefully enable you to enjoy full days out in lovely surroundings, seeing some of the Island's historic landmarks, sampling some locally brewed beers and all with the excuse of keeping fit. What more could anybody want?

This book has been devised so that there is something for everyone and many attractions have been included so that the walks offer a lot of interest. The walks vary from 3 to 10.75 miles but don't let the longer walks deter you. They have been carefully selected so that they give you a day out with plenty to see and do, so there is no rush.

The Island has a lot of coastal paths which are sadly being eroded, some at a fast pace. Care must be taken when walking by the cliffs, especially if you have children with you and any detours observed. The directions given on those walks mention this fact and describe alternate routes for when this occurs.

There is also a wide variety of wildlife, especially coastal bird's but the Island is also one of the only places left in the UK that is home to the red squirrel. They are much easier to see than you might expect but very difficult to get that perfect photograph.

Routes and Maps

The walks are graded from one to

three boots — easy to more challenging. All of the walks are circular so you conveniently end up back where you started. All the start points are by a country pub so refreshments are available at the start or end (or both) of each walk. Sketchmaps are included, and the routes have been described in fine detail, but a compass and Ordnance Survey map is always recommended wherever you go walking.

Parking

Parking points have been given for each walk, some of which may refer to the featured pub's car park. Please, only park there with permission and thank them by frequenting the pub. The parking was free on all the walks at the time of writing but please check to make sure that charges have not been introduced over time or any restrictions imposed.

Public Transport

The main bus company on the Island is Southern Vectis who run an extensive service that covers most of the Island. For information phone: 01983 532373 or visit www.islandbuses.info

Trains

The 8½ miles of passenger railway on the Island is operated by Island Line Trains, on a route serving Shanklin, Lake, Sandown, Brading, Smallbrook Junction and Ryde Pier Head (where there is a connection with the Wightlink high-speed catamaran service from Portsmouth Harbour). The actual rolling stock consists of lovingly cared for ex-London Underground trains and they operate from early morning (starting around 6am) until after midnight. Throughout most of the day, there are two trains an hour. The company has a wide range of ticket types. Phone 01983 812591 or visit: www.island-line.co.uk for details.

Cowes Chain Ferry

There is a chain ferry (also known as the floating bridge) for transporting foot passengers and vehicles across the River Medina from East to West Cowes and vice versa. For further information including current crossing times and prices, contact the Ferry Manager on 01983 293041.

Enjoy the walks and don't forget your camera!

Key to Symbols Used

Level of difficulty:

Easy 🍃

Fair 🍃🍃

More challenging 🍃🍃🍃

Map symbols:

🚗 Park & start

——— Road

----- Footpath

■ Building / Town

+ Church

🍺 Pub

Walk Locations

Cowes

Newport

Alum Bay

ISLE OF WIGHT

Bembridge

Niton

2 1 3 4 5 6 8 7 9 10

1 Freshwater

Three pubs and a view of Hurst Castle and Lighthouse. This is a fairly easy going walk with no steep hills. Apart from the pubs, the highlight is is a good view of Hurst Castle and Lighthouse.

The walk starts by a lovely pub and a church where there is a memorial to the poet Alfred, Lord Tennyson. The walk then goes cross country and on to a viewing point in Fort Victoria Country Park where you get a lovely view of Hurst Castle and Lighthouse over on the mainland. The return journey takes you to two more pubs.

Level: 🥾🥾
Length: 7.25 miles (11.7 km)
Terrain: This is a fairly easy going walk. Any hills are minor and none of them steep.
Stiles: 4
Park & start: On-road parking by the Red Lion.
Postcode: PO40 9BP
Start ref: SZ 346872
Refreshments: Featured pubs

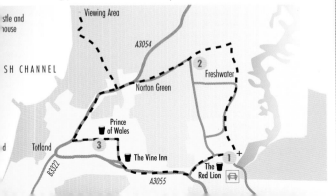

The Red Lion

1 Turn left between the pub and the church on Footpath F1. Go through a bridle gate and continue with the graveyard on the right and then on between wire fences and through another bridle gate out to a lane.

Go ahead up the lane on Footpath F1 with limited views of the River Yar some distance away to your right. Where the lane ends with a farm directly in front of you go left through

All Saints

A marble memorial commemorating Alfred, Lord Tennyson

ALL SAINTS – FRESHWATER
All Saints church is medieval and is one of the oldest churches on the Island. Inside the church there is a marble memorial commemorating Alfred, Lord Tennyson who lived on the Island.

a gate and turn right along the field edge, still on Footpath F1. In the field corner, go through a bridle gate, down between a narrow band of trees and through another bridle gate. Turn left on Footpath F1 and climb gently up the wide track which curves to the right and descends.

At the bottom there are two gates ahead of you which you do not go through but instead you go left over a stile in the wire fence on Footpath F8 – Norton Green. Go diagonally left across the field on a faint path to the far left corner. Go through the wide gap and ahead along the left field edge to a gate in sight. Do not go through this gate but continue with the gate and wire fence on your right. Cross the stile ahead out to a road.

HURST CASTLE AND LIGHTHOUSE

Hurst Castle is at the seaward end of a shingle spit that extends 1.5 miles out from Milford-On-Sea which means that it is only three-quarters of a mile from the Island. The Castle was built by Henry VIII as one of a chain of coastal fortresses and was completed in 1544. Charles I was imprisoned here in 1648 before being taken to London to his trial and execution.
Hurst Point Lighthouse guides ships through the hazardous western approaches to the Solent, showing the line of approach through the Needles Channel. It is said that a light was first shown on Hurst Point as early as 1733 but the first Trinity House record relates to a meeting of shipmasters and merchants in 1781 to approve the terms of a formal petition to Trinity House for lights in the neighbourhood of the Isle of Wight.

2 Go ahead up the road opposite (Colwell Road – not signed) passing a sign for "Norton Green". Follow the road to the end and turn left along Hill Lane then right down Monks Lane. Go down the lane and follow it uphill until you reach the entrance to Linstone Chine Holiday Park ahead. Just before the entrance to the park go right along

Hurst Castle and Lighthouse

the Coastal Path and follow the winding path around the complex and soon enter Fort Victoria Country Park. Almost immediately you reach an information board by a viewing bench where you get a lovely view of Hurst Castle and Lighthouse.

Return the same way back to the entrance to Linstone Chine Holiday Park and go left back down Monks

Lane/Coastal Path and follow it all the way back to the road at the end. Turn right along Colwell Road and follow it for quite some distance until you turn left into Colwell Lane which is opposite Colwell Common on the right. Follow this quiet lane until you reach the Prince of Wales pub on the right.

 Leave the pub and turn right continuing on along Colwell

Lane/Silcome Lane to the end. Turn right along the High Street and follow it down to the end. At the end, go left and The Vine Inn is on the left.

Leave the pub, turn left along School Green Road and follow it to a mini roundabout at the end. Turn left up Hooke Hill and where it bends left go ahead along Church Place back to the Red Lion pub.

The Prince of Wales

The Vine Inn

2 Norton

*Three pubs, Fort Victoria and Yarmouth wooden pier.
This is one of the shortest and easiest walks featured.
There are good sea views, numerous pubs to choose
from and you can explore Yarmouth.*

Yarmouth Castle ■ Wooden Pier
The Kings Head
Lifeboat Station 3 ▪ Bugle Inn
Wheatsheaf Inn
A3054
River Yar
Norton

The walk starts at the large car park at Fort Victoria with all its attractions which you can visit at the start or end of your walk. The walk goes along the seafront to Yarmouth where you can frequent the pubs, have something to eat, visit Yarmouth castle, go along the wooden pier, get a close-up view of the lifeboat at the harbour, and explore the shops. Look out for the small areas of interest that can easily be missed like the commemorative plaques on the wall of the Old Town Hall and the stone carving of the fish by the harbour.

Level:
Length: 3 miles (4.8 km)
Terrain: Level, easy walking.
Stiles: 0
Park & start: Free car park at Fort Victoria.
Postcode: PO41 0RR
Start ref: SZ 339898
Refreshments: Featured pubs and various in Yarmouth.

1 From the free car park at Fort Victoria go down to the beach and look over to your left for a good view of Hurst Castle and Lighthouse.

Turn right along the beach passing the Boathouse Lunch & Tea Gardens on the right. Go along the beach until

FORT VICTORIA

Fort Victoria was a single tier battery with defensible barracks built in the 1850s and later used as a submarine mining centre and training area for military purposes. The larger barrack blocks were demolished in 1969 but the sea-facing casemates were not and this is now all that remains of the Fort.

you continue on the concrete promenade next to the sea. Pass the Norton Grange Coastal Resort on the right and continue to the end of the promenade. Take a couple of paces to the right and continue on a gravel path and in 30 yards, just before a "Norton Spit" information board, go right at the "Coastal Path" sign up to a main road.

Turn left along the road crossing over to the right hand pavement as soon as possible. Follow this road into Yarmouth crossing the New Yar Bridge, so called because it crosses the River Yar and pass the harbour and lifeboat station on the left; it is very likely that you will get a close up view of a lifeboat. Arrive at a bus shelter next to the mini roundabout. From the bus shelter cross the road and go up a "No Entry" road opposite. You can see the Wheatsheaf Inn on the left.

The Wheatsheaf Inn

(2) Leave the inn and turn left to the end of the road next to St James's church on the right. Turn left passing the Old Town Hall on the left with commemorative plaques on the outside front wall including one for Queen Elizabeth II who visited Yarmouth on 27 July 1965. Continue down the road to The Bugle Coaching Inn on the right.

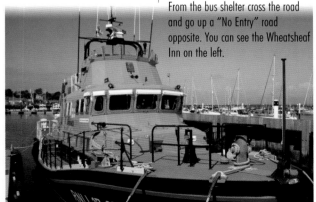

The Bugle Inn

Leave the inn and turn right to the end of the road to the wooden pier which is to the right of a café. There is a small toll to pay to go up the pier but it's only about 30p and you get a good sea view of Yarmouth Castle on the left. Leave the pier and return back towards The Bugle Coaching Inn. Turn right opposite it to The Kings Head pub on the left and the entrance to Yarmouth Castle opposite the pub. The castle opening times are 11am – 4pm between 1 April and 30 September.

(3) When you have finished exploring Yarmouth return to the bus shelter by the mini round-about. Continue ahead along the main road and cross the New Yar Bridge. Cross over to the left hand pavement and continue until you reach Gasworks

YARMOUTH WOODEN PIER

Yarmouth Pier was built in 1876 and is the longest timber pier in England still open to the public. The pier is the only one left in the British Isles that is totally constructed from wood, apart from bolts, screws and such like that hold it together. There is a small toll to pay on entering the pier which helps towards restoration and maintenance costs.

Lane on the left where you cross back over to the right hand pavement. At the left hand bend ahead turn right beside a gate signed "Coastal Path"; do not go ahead along the private drive. Go down to the seafront and turn left signed "Coastal Footpath". Go along a gravel path and in 30 yards step to the right and go ahead along the concrete promenade next to the sea and retrace your outward path to arrive back at Fort Victoria. Here you can visit the Marine Aquarium, Model Railway, Planetarium and Underwater Archaeology Centre.

The Kings Head

3 Calbourne

Two pubs and Winkle Street. At 10.75 miles this is a more challenging walk but there are no steep hills. There is a pub at the start and a second pub conveniently mid-way.

This walk passes the famous Winkle Street, a view on many an Island souvenir and calendar, right at the start then continues cross country for the rest of the walk apart from a few quiet lanes. Also, early on in the walk, there is an opportunity to do a short detour to Calbourne Mill but you could just as easily drive there after you finish.

Level: 🥾 🥾 🥾
Length: 10.75 miles (17.3 km)
Terrain: A few hills but only a couple of short sections are steep.
Stiles: 16 and 2 awkward, heavy gates on Section 4 just past the farm.
Park & start: Limited on street parking opposite the Sun Inn in Lynch Lane.
Postcode: PO30 4JA
Start ref: SZ 426869
Refreshments: Featured pubs

17

The Sun Inn

1 From the Sun Inn go down Lynch Lane opposite passing the Old Village Pump and church on the left. Just past the church turn right into Winkle Street.

Go along the famous Winkle Street and continue on Footpath CB15 with the Caul Bourne stream on the left; the Caul Bourne giving its name to Calbourne. Cross a stile and go diagonally right on Footpath CB13 – Calbourne Mill. Cross the stile in the far right corner next to a gate and go

WINKLE STREET
Winkle Street is a picturesque row of cottages famously seen on many photographs and postcards of the Island. Winkle Street faces the village stream from which the village takes its name – the Caul Bourne. The stream used to power five mills just to the north of the town.

ahead to cross another stile to the left of the farm buildings. Go ahead on the enclosed path, cross an access drive and go over another stile. Go ahead across the field to the right of a house and cross a stile in the far corner. Cross another stile and go down some steps to a road. (Here you can detour about 250 yards left down the fairly quiet road to Calbourne Water Mill on the right taking care as there is no pavement. Return back to this stile to continue the walk.)

2 Turn right up the road taking care as there is no pavement. In about 130 yards at a junction, go over the stile to the left of a 3-way road sign in the opposite hedgerow. Go ahead with the hedgerow on your right and cross a stile in the corner.

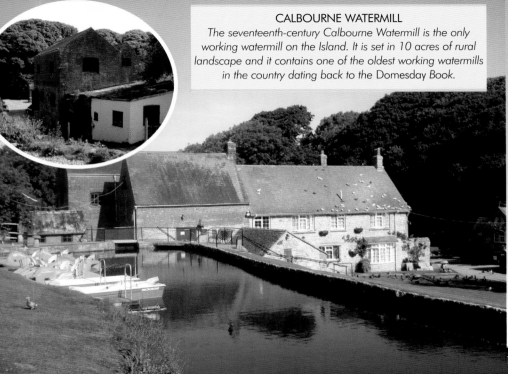

CALBOURNE WATERMILL
The seventeenth-century Calbourne Watermill is the only working watermill on the Island. It is set in 10 acres of rural landscape and it contains one of the oldest working watermills in the country dating back to the Domesday Book.

Follow the left field edge next to hedgerow on the left and be very careful to avoid the rabbit holes. Cross a stile and go around the left field edge with hedgerow on your left; the grass can get a bit long and wet in this field. Cross a stile in the far left corner out to a lane.

Turn left for a few paces then turn right up steps and ahead along Footpath CB10. Continue on this enclosed path crossing 3 plank bridges out into a field. Follow the left edge of this huge field, pass a large dip on the left and when you reach the far side go over a stile next to a gate at a footpath sign to reach a lane. Turn left up the lane towards Sandpits Farm and just before it go right over a stile.

Follow Footpath CB25 down the left edge of the field soon with hedgerow on the left. Cross a small plank bridge and continue to a stile in the hedgerow in the far corner. Cross the stile and follow the left field edge with trees on the left. Go to the very far left corner, go right for 5 yards then go left through a small gap into the next field and continue ahead following the left field edge. From quite some distance away you can see a sign in the far left corner. Go to the sign and turn right for 40 yards then turn left through a wide gap with ponds on either side and ahead next to trees on the left. Cross an access track and continue beneath power lines to reach a stile in the far corner. Cross the stile, go over a plank bridge and ahead along a

clear path through woodland to arrive at a wide track.

Go left on the "Public Bridleway" and in about 150 yards just before a "No

Blackmith's Arms

Entry" sign ahead follow the track around to the right. Just follow this track until you reach a junction at a house called "Watchingwell" which used to be an old railway station and

still has a railway styled name plate. Go right on Footpath N149 – Betty Haunt Lane and after a while the track climbs to pass Great Park House on the left. Continue ahead on the concrete drive until you reach Betty Haunt Lane, not signed. Turn right up the quiet lane and at the end is the welcoming Blacksmith's Arms on the left.

 3 Leave the pub and go up Footpath N197 opposite. Climb steadily beneath trees and in 30 yards where the path forks take the right (ahead) hand path up to a gate. Go through the gate and ahead up the right field edge. In the far field corner go left for 15 yards to a 3-way signpost then go right on Old Highway N136a – Tennyson Trail. Follow the wide track between

hedgerows and then just hedgerow on the right. Where the hedgerow ends at a set of gates, go right through a gate and across a field signed as "Public Footpath".

Follow the direction of the footpath sign across the field to two gates. Go through the gates and ahead down the left field edge. Follow a partially overgrown and faint path to the far left corner and cross a stile. Go down through trees and over a gate or stile (the stile was totally broken at the time of writing). Turn left and follow the left field edge and go through a wide farm gate at the far end of the field. Immediately after passing through the gate turn right on a faint path and go up through trees, over a stile and out to a lane.

4 Turn left along the lane and follow it around to the right. When you reach the TV masts on the right go left through the farm on Bridleway N203. Go through a wide farm gate, ahead and in 15 yards go through another gate to the left of a power pole. Go ahead beneath trees and in 30 yards go through another gate and ahead through trees to reach a gate into a field. Go through the gate and ahead through another gate in 10 yards. Go ahead across the field to a signpost in sight on the far side. At the sign turn right and in the field corner go left through a bridle gate. In a few paces go right through another bridle gate and bear left around a hollow on the left and continue along the top of the field for 70 yards to an interesting wooden structure known as Rowbridge Top Barn; it reminds me of the Sydney Opera House but that's probably just me.

At the barn, or in about 70 yards just in case the barn was to be removed, look over to the right. You will see a valley with a clear winding track at its bottom with trees on the left; that is your onward route. Turn right and walk down the large field and at the bottom of the field you will join with the hedgerow on the right. Go through the gate next to the hedge and ahead along the winding track through the valley. Go through another gate to the right of a cattle grid. Continue on the track and keep ahead and to the right (follow the signage) through Newbarn Farm out to a road. Taking care, turn left along the road and follow it to arrive back at the Sun Inn.

'Sydney Opera House' E

4 **Chale**

Three pubs and two lighthouses. This 9.5 mile walk is more challenging; there are quite a few hills but only a couple of them are steep. The three pubs are lovely, you get very close to both lighthouses and the views are superb.

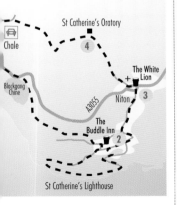

The walk starts near a lovely pub then continues to the cliff-edge path with panoramic views all around. A steep descent down 90 steps takes you towards the new lighthouse then you climb back up to another great pub for well-deserved refreshment. The onward journey takes you to a third lovely pub before you begin your climb uphill to reach the old rocket-shaped oratory. The final part of the walk is thankfully downhill.

Level: 🥾🥾🥾
Length: 9.5 miles (15.3 km)
Terrain: There are quite a few hills but only a couple are steep. There is also one steep descent down a narrow, uneven path with 90 steps that must be done with care at the end of Section 1.
Stiles: 5
Park & start: The Wight Mouse Inn car park, with permission, or limited roadside parking. There is also a small village car park 150 yards before the pub.
Postcode: PO38 2HA
Start ref: SZ 483776
Refreshments: Featured pubs

23

The Wight Mouse Inn

1 Leave The Wight Mouse Inn car park and turn right towards the church. At the end of the road turn left along Blythe Shute then right into The Terrace. Go up the road and very soon go left on Bridleway C15; the sign is on a low wall. Follow the path with a wooden fence on the right to a road at the end. Turn right and follow the road to a roundabout with the entrance to "Blackgang Chine Land of Imagination" on the right.

Go across the roundabout and in 35 yards go right over a stile beside a gate on the "Coastal Path". Go left around the field to the far corner and cross a stile. Go ahead along the woodland path climbing gently to reach a small car park. Turn right through the car park to some steps at the back and continue on the "Coastal Path". Go ahead to the cliff edge with a good view of Blackgang Chine on the right. Turn left and in 15 yards go left through a gap then turn right and follow the cliff edge path heeding any warnings or following any diversions that may be in place due to cliff edge erosion. Just follow this path enjoying the views including St Catherine's Oratory (Pepperpot) on the hill to the left which you will be visiting later. Soon after passing to the right of a

low stone wall you will get very good views of St Catherine's Lighthouse.

Eventually the path reaches a well-placed viewing bench next to a sign-

post. Turn right and follow the footpath down a steep drop with the aid of 90 steps. Take it very slowly as it is steep, narrow in places and uneven. At the bottom go left and immediately

St Catherine's Lighthouse and Knowles Farm

look up on your left to admire your descent. Go to the end of the road and turn right between stone walls and at the end turn left. The Buddle Inn is just up on the left.

② From the pub turn right back along the road and keep ahead at the bend, signposted to St Catherine's lighthouse. Continue down the "Private Road" with a good view of the lighthouse. Stay on the lane as it bears right on Footpath NT37 –

The Buddle Inn

Knowles Farm. As the lane bears left towards the lighthouse go ahead along the access drive to Knowles Farm. Pass to the right of the farm and cross a stile to the left of a gate. Continue ahead along a faint grass path down to the rocky coastline. At the coast go left and follow the coastal path back towards the lighthouse. Just before the lighthouse, cross a stile and head towards the white walls surrounding the lighthouse.

Turn left by the wall and go right through a gate at the end of the wall. Cross the drive and climb over the steps opposite. Turn left with the lighthouse wall on the right. At the end of the wall cross another set of steps on the right and continue ahead

ST CATHERINE'S LIGHTHOUSE

The present tower was constructed in 1838 following the loss of the sailing ship Clarendon on rocks near the site of the present lighthouse. The original height of the lighthouse proved to be too high, as the lantern frequently became mist-capped and in 1875 it was lowered by 13 metres by taking approx. 6 metres out of the upper section and 7 metres out of the middle tier. The lighthouse was automated in 1997 with the keepers leaving on 30 July.

with a hedgerow/stone wall on the left. As you go ahead across the field head diagonally right towards the sea and at the end of the field go through a swing gate next to the cliff edge; this is signposted as "Coastal Path" and is next to a small caravan park.

Enter the caravan park and go left towards the office and car park. At the car park turn left along the access drive and start to climb. Turn right at

the sharp right turn, ignoring a path on the left. Pass a viewing bench on the left where you get your last view back to the lighthouse and in 10 yards go left up a short but steep footpath with steps and a handrail. This is Footpath NT43 and comes out opposite The Buddle Inn. Turn right past the inn and go to the end of the road. Turn left and walk up the right hand pavement following it around to the right and uphill. Pass a church up

on the left and continue down into Niton where you will see the White Lion on the junction in front of you.

(3) Turn left out of the pub and left again to continue down the High Street passing the pub's beer garden on the left. Turn left into Church Street it is not signed but is opposite Rectory Road. At the church gate go right up Pan Lane and follow it as it climbs steadily eventually turning into a track and climbs more steeply; this is also Bridleway NT53. At the end you come to a junction where you turn left and go ahead with a wire fence on the right. Go through a gate and head around towards the mast on the horizon going to the right of a bowl-shaped dip to the top where there is no fence so you can just walk

The White Lion

through. Cross the field towards the mast and soon you will see the top of the Oratory so you can head in that direction. Cross the stile by the trig point and explore the Oratory.

4 Go back to the stile by the trig point but do not cross it. Go left with the wire fence on the right heading towards the Hoy

Monument in the distance. Follow the fence down beside a dip on the left. Immediately after the dip, go diagonally left to a marker post in sight. At the marker post go right as indicated by the blue arrow down between low banks with good views including the church at Chale. Go through a wide gate and continue down between banks.

When the bank on the left ends keep left on a clear path with the church in view ahead. Continue on this path always with the church ahead to reach a farm. Go through a gate and down the track past Chale Farm to a lane. Turn right down the lane to a road where you turn left past the village car park on the right back to The Wight Mouse Inn.

ST CATHERINE'S ORATORY

The Oratory is an ancient example of lighthouse technology. Dating from about 1320, it was erected by Walter de Godeton as an act of penance for plundering wine from the wreck of the St Marie of Bayonne in Chale Bay. Fires were lit in the tower to warn shipping away from the dangerous shore below, and to this day the Oratory serves as a seamark. The Oratory, which resembles the shape of a rocket, is an eight sided tower with a cone roof and four buttresses which look like the rocket's fins.

5 GODSHILL

Three pubs and Godshill village. This 7.75 mile walk is mainly flat but there are a couple of short but steep climbs.

The walk starts by a pub famous for having a maze in its back garden. It continues cross-country for approximately 5 miles before reaching the second pub at Rookley. The onward journey is again cross-country before arriving at the thatched cottages and church at Godshill. The view of the cottages with the top of the church behind it is one of the most famous views on Island souvenirs and calendars. Godshill gets its name from the fact that the church was originally meant to be built at the bottom of the hill but legend has it that each night the stones mysteriously moved uphill to where the church is today. This was taken to be a sign from God hence the name Godshill. The church is one of the most photographed in the country, not just the Island and is regularly open to visitors. Godshill has lots of visitor attractions, a number of shops and another lovely pub to visit.

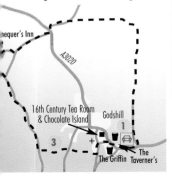

Level: 🐾🐾
Length: 7.75 miles (12.5 km)
Terrain: This is a fairly easy walk along long flat sections. There are a couple of short but fairly steep hills but nothing strenuous.
Stiles: 0
Park & start: Car park opposite The Griffin Inn.
Postcode: PO38 3JD
Start ref: SZ 530816
Refreshments: Featured pubs and various in Godshill.

GODSHILL MODEL VILLAGE
Inset: The real Griffin Inn

The Godshill Model Village is a replica of the villages of Godshill and Shanklin Chine which are two of the oldest tourist areas on the Island. The houses are fantastic replicas of the real buildings, made with sand and cement just like the real thing and the cottages are thatched using authentic materials and methods. Walk around at least twice.

From the car park go to the road by The Griffin Inn and turn left. Follow the road around to the left and after about 200 yards go left on Bridleway GL46 – The Stenbury Trail. Follow the wide track passing Moor Farm and continuing ahead on the same track between fields. After a little over a mile the track goes left as indicated by a blue arrow on a signpost. Follow it around, ignoring a bridleway sign going right, and cross a bridge over a tributary of the River Yar. Continue past Great Budbridge Manor on the left and in 100 yards ignore the bridleway to Godshill and go a few paces further forward and turn left on Bridleway A22 – Rookley.

Follow the gravel track with tall conifers on the left. When the gravel ends continue on the track going left then right around the field edge and continue to arrive at a lane to the right of a house. Turn left down this quiet lane and follow it up to Newport Road. Turn left along the road and cross over as soon as possible to the grass verge opposite. Turn right into Chequers Inn Road and follow this quiet road climbing gradually. Ignore Footpath GL8 on the right and continue ahead. Follow the road as it bends right when opposite Bridleway GL8b on the left and continue to reach a road with The Chequers Inn on the right at Rookley.

Leave the inn and turn left. Do not go along the main road but go 5 yards up Chequers Inn Road and turn right into Bagwich Lane; it is opposite the side of the

The Chequers Inn

*Godshill's thatched
cottages and church*

inn. Climb fairly steeply up this quiet lane passing Southview on the left and the entrance to East View Farm on the right. Continue and pass Bagwich Holiday Cottages and Chestnut Farm on the left and 20 yards past Chestnut Farm go left on Bridleway GL21 — Godshill; the sign is partially hidden in the hedgerow. Go across the field on a faint path; go through a bridle gate and across the next field to a gate in sight in the far right corner. (If the field is full of crops you may have to walk around the right hand edge.)

(3) Go through the gate to a marker post in 5 yards and go left down into woodland. Cross a bridge and follow the path around to the left with a stream on the left and

GODSHILL

The name 'Godshill' is said to originate from the foundations of the local four-teenth-century church which was moved from the bottom of the hill to its present loca-tion at the top of the hill as the stones kept mysteriously moving uphill overnight whilst it was being built. This was taken to be a sign from God that the church should be built on the hill.

then go right past a pond on the left. The path goes around the pond then turns right with a wire fence on the left to reach a road. Cross the road and climb up the field opposite on

Bridleway GL21; Godshill church is ahead and to the left and as you cross the field you can look back on your left at where you have walked. On the far side of the field join a lane and turn left to the much photographed thatched houses and church. This view is common on many of the souvenir items in the gift shops and on Isle of Wight calendars.

Go up the short road towards the thatched cottages on the right and continue through to the church. Go up to the church, it is likely to be open if you want to visit, and turn right down the access path. Go down steps and ahead into Godshill passing a six-teenth-century thatched tea room on the right if you rather a cup of tea instead of an alcoholic beverage and

*Sixteenth-century
tea room*

Chocolate Island if you want to replace some calories.

Turn right down the High Street passing all its attractions. The Taverners is on the left almost opposite the Model Village. Enter the pub by the door at the rear of the car park which takes you into their little shop area before you go through to the bar. Leave the pub and turn left back to The Griffin Inn and the car park.

The Taverners

6 Arreton

Three pubs and Arreton Old Village. This walk is generally level and easy going. There are a number of hills but only one of them is steep. The highlight of this walk, apart from the pubs, is Arreton Old Village which has something for everyone.

The walk starts by a pub which I suggest you visit as it is a lovely establishment and the next one is about 6.5 miles away. The walk goes cross-country eventually reaching the next beautiful thatched pub for a welcoming drink. The onward journey is again cross-country back to Arreton where you must make time to explore the Old Village and frequent the lovely, interesting last pub.

Level: 🥾🥾
Length: 7.75 miles (12.5 km)
Terrain: Most of this walk is generally level. However, there are a number of hills but only one is steep at the end of Section 3.
Stiles: 9
Park & start: Car park next to The White Lion.
Postcode: PO30 3AA
Start ref: SZ 533867
Refreshments: Featured pubs and Arreton Old Village.

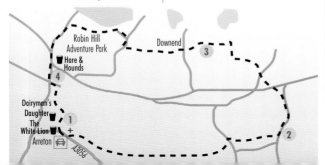

35

The White Lion

Leave the car park and go back to the main road next to The White Lion pub; the next pub is about 6.5 miles away. Go left along the road and turn left into School Lane. Go past the school and ahead with hedgerow on the left. When the hedgerow ends go through a gap and continue with the hedgerow on the right. Soon you automatically contin-ue with the hedgerow back on the left and soon after it ends you arrive at a signpost.

Turn right and in 20 yards turn left on a bridleway. Go ahead along the wide track and just after passing under power lines continue with hedgerow/bushes on the right. Go through a bridle gate and continue ahead on a wide path between fences. On the other side go slightly left and follow the track around to the right with the hedgerow on your right. When the track bends left continue ahead to the field corner and go out to the lane.

Turn left up the lane and turn right past a house on Footpath NC1 – Knighton. Follow the track up and around to the right as it becomes Footpath NC7 – Knighton. Follow the wide path with high trees on the left. When the trees end continue ahead and in 20 yards carry on along a narrow path between wire fences with paddocks either side. Cross a stile and continue on the right hand side of the next fields with trees on the right. In the field corner, walk out to a lane at Knighton.

2 Turn left along the lane passing Knighton Farmhouse on the right and follow the lane as it curves to the left and starts to climb. Just past Footpath NC3 on the right and opposite a forward facing sign for Knighton on the right go left over a stile on Footpath NC2 – Mersley Down. (The sign and stile are partially hidden behind trees and could easily be missed.) Climb diagonally right up across the field as directed by the arrow and aim just to the left of a dead tree on the horizon. Continue past the tree and go over a stile in the far fence out to a road.

Cross the road and go over the stile opposite on Footpath R17 – Rowlands Lane. Cross the field as directed and go over the stile to the left of a gate into Rowlands Lane. Turn right down the lane to a footpath sign in sight. Cross the stile and follow Footpath R15 – Duxmore.

Cross the field to a yellow marker in sight at the left end of a wire fence. Go ahead with the wire fence on the right and enter woodland. Continue on the winding woodland path until you reach a stile on the right next to a gate. Cross the stile and go ahead down the field. Near the bottom keep a hedgerow on the left and follow the narrow path next to an area of newly planted trees. Cross a stile ahead into woodland and follow the path. As soon as the main woodland ends by a marker post and with a brick building in view ahead go left through a gate with an arrow on it. Go across the field following the line of power poles. On the other side continue on the wide track with Duxmore Farm ahead. Follow the track past the farm buildings out to a lane.

Old Village

The Hare and Hounds

3 Turn left along the lane then right. Go through a wide gate and ahead to a crossing lane. Continue ahead through a gap in the opposite hedgerow and go across the field to a gate on the far side. Go through the gate and ahead with hedgerow on the right. Go through a gate and continue next to a wire fence and just before the far field corner go right through a gate as indicated by an arrow near the gate. Go down the field aiming for a gate in the far left corner. Go through the gate and turn right back towards the farm.

Go left through the farm and out through the large gate opposite; there is an arrow on the left gate post. Go ahead up the left access track and in 40 yards go left through a gate next to a power pole, not signed. Go around the left edge of the field walking beneath the power cables. Just after a circle of trees on the right go left through a gate. Walk steeply up through woodland on a clear path with a wire fence on the left. At the end you arrive at a fairly busy road with no pathway. Turn left and walk, with care and on the right hand side, up the road until about 50 yards before the roundabout when it is best to cross back over to the left hand side and continue until you reach the entrance to Robin Hill Adventure Park on the left. Straight after the entrance you reach The Hare and Hounds for well-deserved refreshment.

4 Leave the pub and turn left towards the traffic lights. Go across the lights (not left around the pub) and follow the road again with no pavement; this time it is better to walk on the left as there is a narrow edge by the road that you can step on to. In about 250 yards, opposite Burnt House Lane on the right go left through a gate on Footpath A12 – Arreton. Cross the field on the obvious path although it is faint in places. Just before passing under power lines go right towards an information board.

Pass the board, go down a few steps and go through a gate. Walk down across the field aiming for St George's church ahead. In the field corner, go ahead with a pond on the left to arrive at the church. Walk past the church back to the car park passing Lavender and Lace on the right. Change your boots and leave your bags then visit Arreton Old Village by returning to Lavender and Lace and going along the path to the left of it.

The Dairyman's Daughter

The Dairyman's Daughter is there and easy to find.

ARRETON OLD VILLAGE

Arreton Barns Craft Centre/ Old Village is a real delight. At the Shipwreck Centre you can relive the golden age of ships when sailors struggled against stormy seas to deliver people and goods to their destination. Also, butchers, sweets, glass sculpting, pottery, a large pond etc.

7 Wootton

Three pubs and a creek. This is a longer walk at 8.75 miles but it is generally level and any hills are minor. The walk takes in three lovely pubs and has good views of Wootton Creek.

This walk starts at a car park with a five hour time limit so if you feel you need longer to enjoy this walk and visit the pubs look for alternate parking somewhere in a side street. The walk begins next to Wootton Creek and offers an optional detour for a good view of Fishbourne ferry terminal; it then goes cross-country to reach the lovely Cedars pub. From here the walk continues and crosses the Isle of Wight Steam Railway where if you are very fortunate you may get a close up view of one of the steam trains. Soon you reach the next pub before returning back toward the creek at Wootton and your final pub looking out for Fernhill Ice-House on the way.

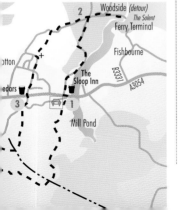

Level: 🐾 🐾
Length: 8.75 miles (14.1 km) — includes the half mile optional detour.
Terrain: Generally quite level any hills are very minor and none strenuous.
Stiles: 5
Park & start: Car park in Brannon Way. NB max stay of five hours; find limited roadside parking if you need more than 5 hours.
Postcode: PO33 4NX
Start ref: SZ 544919
Refreshments: Featured pubs and shops at Wootton.

1 Leave the car park and go back to the High Street. Turn right down the High Street then go left along New Road. (The Sloop Inn is a little further down the High Street beside Wootton Creek if you wish to visit now.)

Follow this road ignoring any side paths or roads and soon after the road curves to the right it opens out and you get some good views of Wootton Creek; unfortunately, there is no dedicated footpath beside the creek. At speed restriction signs the path ends so continue with care. Pass what is currently Creek Gardens Holiday Cottages on the right and continue climbing gently, still on New Road, with a wire fence on the right. As the road levels out pass the entrance to

WOOTTON CREEK
Wootton Creek is a tidal estuary that flows into the Solent on the north coast of the Island. The creek is not navigable south of the bridge and tide controls mean that water is retained south of the bridge most of the time. So south of the bridge the creek is quiet with water birds being fed and north of the bridge it is much busier with plenty of boats to look at.

Little Canada Holiday Village on the right. The road stops at a junction where you can make an optional half mile detour.

The detour takes you to the end of Wootton Creek opposite the Fishbourne ferry terminal. It is signposted to "The Shore" but it is not a beach. I think it is worthwhile for the view, it is easy going and it won't take you long. To do the detour turn right and follow the access road to the

Ferry terminal detour

very end where there is a small gate with a yellow arrow that directs you down a narrow path to the water's edge. It is quite likely that you will see a ferry at Fishbourne or one arriving or leaving. There is also Footpath N157 just before the end of the road that takes you down to the shore which you might like to explore. There is much more of a shore there but it's not one you will really want to walk on although the views are good. Return to the junction of paths after your detour.

(2) To continue take the left (or opposite if you did the detour) path signed Aldene 1/4. Go up the track, pass Aldene on the right and continue climbing very gently between trees. The track arrives at a junction and you continue ahead through a gate on Footpath N99 — Church Road. Go ahead on the enclosed path ducking down if you are tall. Go through a squeeze gate and ahead past a church on the left. At the end turn left past St Edmund's church and then turn right along Church Road — not signed here. Go to the end of this road where you reach traffic lights with The Cedars opposite.

(3) Leave the pub and turn right along Station Road. Go past Fernhill on the left and take the next

turning on the left along Packsfield Lane which is also Bridleway N8. Follow this access road around to the right and then down between trees to the bottom. The path then climbs gently and crosses the Isle of Wight Steam Railway Line. If you are really lucky with your timing you may get a very good view of a steam train passing through to Wootton Station on the right. On the other side of the railway, go right on Bridleway — N6. The path bears left, climbs between trees and ends directly opposite The Woodman Arms. Turn right to the road and left to the pub.

4 Leave the pub, turn right then right again back into Packsfield Lane on Bridleway N5. This time do not turn left down Packsfield Lane South but go ahead with the pub garden on your right. Follow this access road which soon bears left and runs parallel with a lane on the right. Ignore a bridleway on the left, continue for 30 yards and turn right at a bridleway sign to the right of a large house; this is Littletown Lane but it is not signed. Go past houses and just past the last house go left over a stile on Footpath N2.

Go ahead across the field on a faint path and cross a stile in sight. Go across the next field walking between the two power poles to a stile on the opposite side in sight. Cross the stile and go ahead in the direction of the yellow arrow on a very faint path. Cross a stile and go up through wood-land. Cross a stile and continue around the right edge of a field with the railway line away to the left. Cross a stile on the right just before the field corner, turn left on Bridleway N1 and follow the track around and down to cross the railway.

On the other side of the railway take the left track and follow it ignoring any side paths, gates or stiles. This is a long and winding path but keep a look out for the "Fernhill Ice-House" on the left at the edge of the woodland; there is an information board telling you all about it. It is easily missed walking from this direction but it is opposite a stile on the right and at the time of writing there was a large tree trunk lying on the ground in front of it.

The Woodman Arms

FERNHILL ICE-HOUSE

Ice houses were generally built underground and were used for storing winter-cut ice blocks from nearby lakes. The blocks would have been used at the grand Fernhill House which burnt to the ground in 1938.

FERNHILL ICE-HOUSE

Just keep going on this obvious and fairly wide track and eventually you will go through a bridle gate to the right of Fernhill Farm. Continue ahead down to Wootton Creek and turn left to The Sloop Inn ahead. Visit the Inn or turn left up the High Street and left into Brannon Way back to the car park within your five hour parking limit.

The Sloop Inn

8 Newchurch

Two pubs and Amazon World. This 7.5 mile walk is hilly but none of them are steep. The walk has two lovely pubs and the opportunity to visit Amazon World which has a fantastic collection of animals that is of interest to both young and old.

The walk starts by The Pointer Inn then continues cross-country, along quiet lanes and there is some road-side walking. You eventually reach Amazon World which you can visit or continue for a very short distance for refreshment at The Fighting Cocks pub. The return part of the walk is over similar terrain as before.

Level: 🐾 🐾
Length: 7.5 miles (12.1 km)
Terrain: This is a hilly walk but none of them are very steep or strenuous
Stiles: 1
Park & start: Car park in School Lane.
Postcode: PO36 0NL
Start ref: SZ 562853
Refreshments: Featured pubs and Amazon World.

1. From the car park go back to the High Street. Turn right along the High Street to The Pointer Inn. Do not go down the hill by the inn but take the upper path that runs to the left of the church on Footpath NC46. At the end of the churchyard by a gate turn right with the low wall on

your left and just before a graveyard ahead of you go left through a gap in the wall, down three steps and turn right along a wide track. Go ahead past the graveyard on the right and continue along a left field edge. At a 3-way signpost on the left, go right on Footpath NC12 – Alverstone Garden Village. Go across the field on a clear path reaching two ornate stone benches in about 30 yards. Turn left at the benches and follow the path down. Where the path forks by a marker post go ahead, gradually curving to the right. At the bottom go ahead beside a post displaying a map, go into woodland and across a small bridge. Climb up the other side going right at a junction and continuing to climb the winding path to a stile. Go over the stile and turn right. Go through a wide gate and ahead to the right of an outbuilding. Go ahead through two more gates between the farm buildings. On the other side of the farm, go through a wide gate and ahead up the access track to a lane at the end; this is also Footpath NC11b.

2 Turn left along Skinner's Hill, not signed, for some distance to reach a road junction. Turn right along Alverstone Road, not signed and follow the residential road passing Queen Bower Dairy on the right.

Amazon World

AMAZON WORLD

Amazon World will appeal to adults as well as children. You can learn about conservation and rainforests but to most people coming face to face with some of the world's most unusual, beautiful and endangered creatures will be the highlight of their visit. Some of the creatures cannot be seen anywhere else in the UK or even Europe.

Continue, turning right into Forest Road which you follow to its end. Go ahead along Watery Lane and follow it to a lane at the end. Turn left along the lane soon reaching a Garden Centre and Amazon World on the right.

Visit Amazon World or continue to the end of the road. Turn right along the main A3056 to The Fighting Cocks on the left.

3 Leave the pub and turn left along the main road soon passing Footpath A21 and a garage on the left. Now you have to look carefully for your next footpath as it is partially obscured by trees. Not too long after passing the garage on the left look for a newish house on the right that has a brick wall at the front and weatherboards on its upper floor. Footpath A20 is to the right of this house. (At the time of writing it was the last house but more houses might be built.)

Follow the enclosed path with

nurseries on the left. Go through a gate, across a drive and continue ahead between wire fences. On the far side continue ahead through a belt of woodland and then between paddocks. On the other side of the paddocks go half left ahead (to the right of a yellow square on a gate post) on a wide track between fences. 5 yards after the fence on the right ends go right on a narrow path across a field and beneath power cables. On the far side you reach Wackland Lane, not signed, where you turn right now walking with the power cables about 2 yards to your right. Follow this lane to the end where it meets Winford Road, not signed. Turn left along Winford Road and follow it to the car park and pub back at the start.

The Fighting Cocks

9 St Helen's

Three pubs and three offshore forts. This walk is fairly easy – there are a couple of hills but they are not too demanding. The walk goes along beaches, around a bay, through minor woodland and across countryside and offers some lovely views.

The walk starts by The Vine Inn then heads down to the ruins of St Helen's church with the first off-shore fort behind it. It continues along a beach, though minor woodland to reach Seagrove Bay with views of the other two off-shore forts and where you can enjoy a drink at the Old Fort Bar Café. The walk continues to the Roadside Inn then cross-country back to the start.

Level: 🥾🥾

Length: 6.5 miles (10.5 km)

Terrain: Mainly flat. There are a couple of hills but they are not too demanding. Watch your footing through Priory Woods as it is very uneven.

Stiles: 2

Park & start: On street parking by The Vine Inn.

Postcode: PO33 1UJ

Start ref: SZ 627890

Refreshments: Featured pubs and other shops / cafés en-route.

1 Leave The Vine Inn and turn left along the road with a green on the right. Continue past the green and where the road bends left go ahead down Duver Road. Go to the end of this road and where it bends right go straight ahead signed to the Baywatch Beach Café. Immediately ahead you see the ruins of St Helen's church and behind it out at sea is the first of the three forts — St Helen's Fort.

The Vine Inn

ST HELEN'S FORT
The fort was built between 1867 and 1880 as a result of the Royal Commission to protect St Helen's anchorage. It suffered badly from subsidence which forced many changes to the plans. It was offered for sale in 2003 but any private resident would not have any access to local authority services, although it has its own artesian well.

2 At the ruins turn left and walk along the seafront at Priory Bay with Priory Woods on the left. Just before the onward beach path becomes blocked by rocks go left up steps into Priory Woods. At the top of the steps go right and follow the woodland path. Climb more steps and go down steps opposite. Follow this woodland path around Priory Bay via steps and along walk-boards etc. Take care along here as some of the boards are uneven or broken and there are also a lot of tree roots that can trip you up.

Stay on this path with views through to the beach. At a yellow arrow go left up steps and turn right at the top. Follow the obvious path as directed by more yellow arrows and soon you are

NO MAN'S LAND FORT

No Man's Land Fort was built in the Solent between 1867 and 1880 to protect Portsmouth. It is 2.2 km off the coast, cost £462,500 and is almost identical to Horse Sand Fort behind it. It is now a luxury home/hospitality centre for high-paying guests due to its privacy. It has an indoor swimming pool and two helipads. The 1972 Doctor Who serial "The Sea Devils" used the fort for filming several scenes.

directed down steps to the beach. Turn left along the sandy beach with the Spinnaker Tower at Portsmouth in view ahead and you will also see the other two offshore forts. The left hand fort closest to the shore is No Man's Land Fort and the other is Horse Sand Fort.

When you reach more rocks on the beach it is possible to continue and walk around Seagrove Bay on the other side but if the tide is blocking you there are more steps on the left just before the rocks. On the other side of the rocks go left around the bay using the wooden walkway if necessary; this is where you will come out if you had to go via the steps. Walk around Seagrove Bay on the upper wall and then the beach. Soon you

Old Fort Bar Café

will have to leave the beach when your onward path is blocked but you can soon re-join it. A little further on there is a low wall on the left which it is recommended you use as a bit further on there are large uneven rocks on the beach that are best avoided.

Leave the beach where the low wall ends via a ramp to a road. You can see the Seaview Hotel up the hill to your left but you need to continue on the road ahead next to the beach. In

50 yards you reach the Old Fort Bar Café.

 Turn right out of the bar and return the 50 yards to the ramped beach exit. This time go right up the High Street, not signed and pass the Seaview Hotel on the right. Go to the top of the High Street and continue to the top of Old Seaview Road. Just past Solent View Road you join the B3340, Seaview Lane. Go left up the hill and at the top you arrive next to a triangular green on the right. Continue on the road ahead, Nettlestone Green, and in 40 yards you reach The Roadside Inn on the left.

 Leave the pub and turn left passing Orchard Road on the

left. Take the next turning left into Caws Avenue and immediately go right into Priory Drive. Follow this road to the end and continue to the right of Gully Road; do not go left along Gully Road. Walk up the rising access road with a drainage ditch on the right at first. Continue until you reach the entrance to the Priory Hotel ahead.

Do not go through the entrance but turn right on a wide track. Cross a stile ahead and go across the field with hedgerow on the left. Cross a stile to the left of a gate and continue ahead; there is a good view of the Lifeboat Station over to the left. On the other side you arrive at a road. Take a few paces right then go left along the opposite footpath on a long enclosed path. Eventually this path goes to the right of a school and out to houses. Turn left along a road then right to arrive back at The Vine Inn on the right.

The Roadside Inn

10 Bembridge

Three pubs, a harbour, lifeboat station and St Helen's ruins. Although this is a 9.5 mile walk it is mainly flat and the few climbs are not steep. There is so much to see including three lovely pubs; one with the façade shaped like a boat with porthole windows.

The walk starts next to the fantastic Crab & Lobster pub then continues along the beach to reach a lifeboat station which you can visit and get close up to the lifeboat. From here you continue along quite a dramatic coastline until you go around Bembridge Harbour to reach The Pilot Boat Inn shaped like a boat. The onward journey takes you across St Helen's

Duver to reach the ruins of St Helen's church and its association with Lord Nelson. The walk then heads inland to reach the lovely Ye Olde Village Inn before returning to the start.

Level: 🥾🥾

Length: 9.25 miles (14.9 km)

Terrain: Mostly flat with the first section being along a pebble beach. A couple of climbs but neither is steep.

Stiles: 0

Park & start: Car park at the end of Forelands Field Rd through a "Private" gate.

Postcode: PO35 5TR

Start ref: SZ 655873

Refreshments: Featured pubs, cafés and shops.

From the back of the car park turn left without going down the steps. Follow the "Coastal Path" sign between a wall and fence and very soon the The Crab & Lobster pub is on the left.

Go down the steps as directed and at the bottom turn left and walk either on the upper wall or along the beach. At a ramp coming down from the left you will have to walk along the beach. Continue ahead soon with the New Lifeboat Station in view.

Bembridge lifeboat

The Pilot Boat Inn

Continue past the Lifeboat Station, it is usually open for visiting and just keep going, curving gently round to the left to arrive at the harbour entrance.

Turn left and walk around the edge of the Harbour. When you reach a "Private Members" building ahead go left past a café to a road. Turn left along the road passing the Palmer Memorial Drinking Fountain. Just past the fountain you

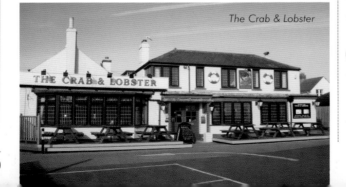

The Crab & Lobster

ST HELEN'S DUVER

*St Helen's Duver is reached via a long causeway.
The Duver was once the location of the Island's first golf
course but it is now a popular beach. Interesting wildlife
species include burrowing digger wasps, wasp spiders
and water birds.*

arrive at Station Road next to the boat-shaped pub, The Pilot Boat Inn.

3 From the pub return to the drinking fountain and follow the road round passing the Toll Gate Café and harbour on the right. Soon you pass some lovely houseboats and the "Overboard" café which is actually on a boat. At the far end of the harbour turn right into the entrance for Bembridge Marina. Go to the far side, cross a bridge and go ahead for 15 yards to a road. Turn right along the road and follow Footpath R108. Go left beside the harbour then right with the harbour on the right. Turn left around large sheds and follow Footpath R86 across the causeway to an area known as The Duver.

St Helen's ruins

On Saturday 14th September 1805, Admiral Lord Nelson boarded HMS Victory lying at anchor off St Helens near to this spot. HMS Victory, with HMS Euryalus in company, sailed the following morning, Sunday 15th September, to join the Fleet off Cadiz prior to the Battle of Trafalgar, 21st October 1805.

ST HELEN'S RUINS

The tower is what remains of St Helen's church which was built early in the twelfth century; the tower dates from about 1220. The church ceased to be used in 1703 when the tower was bricked up and turned into the seamark which remains today. The derelict church became a source of Holy Stones which were taken by sailors to scrub down the decks of wooden ships.

Follow the causeway to the far side and go straight ahead across grass then slightly to the right to join a tarmac road. Turn left along the road and continue ahead ignoring a right turn towards a car park. The road bends left then right and at the next left bend you go right signed as Parking and Baywatch Beach Café. The ruins of St Helen's church are immediately in front of you and behind it out at sea is St Helen's Fort.

 Return back to the same road and continue ahead at the "Give Way" sign passing Old Church Lodge on the left. Climb up the hill to a junction at the top and continue ahead along Upper Green Road. In 50 yards, go left opposite the Community Centre with a green on the right. Turn

left into Mill Road which is also signed to Old Mill Holiday Park. Descend and pass caravans, soon with a good view of the causeway you walked along earlier; this is why I have taken you back this way.

At the bottom you arrive back at the harbour. Go right past flats on the left, then turn left back over the bridge that is in sight. Walk back out to the main road, turn left and head back to The Pilot Inn. To the left of the inn, go up Pump Lane which is also Footpath BB34 – Dulcie Avenue. Go up the gravel access road between houses and at a junction go right which is Dulcie Avenue, not signed. Go along this gravel access road to reach a road at the end. Turn left along the road and then right passing between shops. Continue ahead soon passing a war memorial on the right and in another 60 yards reaching Ye Olde Village Inn on the left.

5 Leave the pub and turn right, back the way you came. Pass the war memorial and go ahead up a "No Entry" road. Turn right into Foreland Road and follow it to the very end opposite The Windmill Hotel. Turn left along Lane End Road then right into Walls Road. Pass a fire station on the left and then turn left into Crossway. Go to the end and turn right into Egerton Road and go to the end. Turn left then right into Forelands Field Road and go to the end where you will find the Crab & Lobster and the car park.

Ye Olde Village Inn